the wisdom of Black Spirituality, especially
the pra              ..." – waiting on God –
as a cc

On the                                        s
in dark                                       ne.
Thoug
watch                                         sleep,
leavir                                        st
suffering. The forty days                     s
the opportunity to respond differently and
wait with Jesus in his anguish and isolation.
Making space to watch and pray – together
and as individuals – can help us rest and be
restored by God's presence. And it can also
help us become more aware of a suffering
world that desperately needs us to share
God's healing with those we encounter.

These *Watch and Pray* reflections challenge
us to seek God in both familiar and
unfamiliar places: in darkness and in quiet;
in movement and migration; in the healing
and transforming work of the Spirit; in the
weeping of Holy Week and in the joy of
Easter morning.

Our prayer is that this Lent may bring
you not only waiting but healing, not only
rest but renewed hope. May we all be
encouraged and supported as we journey
together. And may we meet and be
transformed by the Lord of lords, whose
day is near.

# Acknowledgements

**_Watch and Pray: Wisdom and hope for Lent and life_ is the Church of England's theme for Lent 2024.**

These daily reflections have been inspired and informed by the Archbishop of Canterbury's 2024 Lent Book, _Tarry Awhile: Wisdom from Black Spirituality for people of faith_ (SPCK) by **Dr Selina Stone**, Postdoctoral Research Associate in Theological Education at Durham University with Common Awards.

The reflections have been written by **The Revd Dr Carlton Turner**, Anglican Tutor in Contextual Theology and Mission Studies at the Queens Foundation Birmingham.

The Church House Publishing and the Church of England Communications teams are grateful to **SPCK Publishing** for their collaboration, which helps us maximise the resources offered to churches, discussion groups and individuals. And we are most grateful to Selina Stone for working closely with Carlton Turner to ensure close coordination between the Archbishop's Lent Book and the wider range of resources.

Details of the Lent book and the full range of resources to support this year's Lent theme can be found at **cofe.io/WatchAndPray**

# Contents

# How to use this booklet

***Watch and Pray: Wisdom and hope for Lent and life*** encourages us to wait expectantly for God to meet us and sustain us through life's storms and trials.

This booklet contains 40 reflections, one for each of the forty days in Lent, which begins on Ash Wednesday (which falls on 14 February 2024) and ends on Easter Eve (30 March 2024), plus one for Easter Day.

You can use it on its own, but my hope is that those who are also reading Selina Stone's *Tarry Awhile: Wisdom from Black Spirituality for people of faith* (SPCK) – either individually or as part of a discussion group – will find it helpful, too.

For each week there is:

- A **theme** which corresponds to the chapters of the 2024 Lent book
- A **brief introduction** to the theme and readings for the week
- A **simple prayer** for use through the week.

This year's reflections draw on the wisdom of Black Spirituality, particularly the practice of "tarrying" (waiting) as a community to draw closer to Jesus and to each other. The weekly themes mirror the chapters of the Lent book, exploring the idea of "tarrying" with God from different perspectives.

For each day (Monday to Saturday) there are daily reflections which offer:

- A **theme**
- An original **illustration**
- A **short passage from the Bible**
- A **reflection** on the theme and reading
- A **challenge** both to watch (notice or reflect) and to pray.

Finally, there are a range of suggestions for **Going Further**.

There is also a daily ***Watch and Pray*** challenge for children available in the accompanying booklet ***Watch and Pray: A Lent journey for children***. This offers a weekly reading and prayer, together with 40 daily activities to help children and families explore together the idea of waiting with and for God as we prepare for Easter.

This booklet will be accompanied by daily social media posts from Ash Wednesday to Easter Day, together with a wide range of video and other free digital resources for individuals, groups and churches available via **cofe.io/WatchAndPray**

Carlton Turner

**Start of Lent**

# Waiting in Darkness

**Watch and Pray invites us all to wait expectantly for God this Lent, and to draw on Black Spirituality in search of new wisdom and hope even in times of struggle and trial.** We begin the journey waiting with – and searching for – God in darkness.

## Prayer for the Week

*Lord, grant us the faith to wait together in darkness and uncertainty – for it is there we will find you. May we come to know you this Lent in ways we have not yet discovered or even imagined. Amen.*

# Waiting with Jesus

## Read

*"Then Jesus went with them to a place called Gethsemane; and he said to his disciples, 'Sit here while I go over there and pray.' "*

**Matthew 26.36-38**

*Watch and Pray* invites us all to wait expectantly for God this Lent, and to draw on Black Spirituality in search of new wisdom and hope.

The spiritual practice known as "tarrying" is a prominent aspect of many Black – especially Pentecostal – congregations. "Tarrying" is a time of waiting on God which involves the whole community. It encourages us to encounter God both as individuals and together. As we wait, we pray for our own needs, as well as those of our neighbour.

"Tarrrying" also encourages us to watch, paying attention to matters we might push under the rug to deal with "another time". Doing so might feel overwhelming. But as we sit in the presence of God who looks upon us with delight, we find ourselves waiting with and for Jesus, who is familiar with our weaknesses.

# Watch

Notice any worries or feelings you might be afraid to deal with as we begin Lent.

# and pray

today by setting aside time to hold these before God – and wait.

# Waiting in darkness

## Read

"Jesus said to Peter, 'So, could you not stay awake with me one hour? Stay awake and pray that you may not come into the time of trial ...' "

**Matthew 26.39-46**

Yesterday we explored the Black spiritual practice of "tarrying" (waiting) as a community to draw closer to Jesus and to each other. Combining exuberant singing, fervent prayer and quiet lament, such services typically take place at night and can last for several hours.

Such "tarrying" services are rooted in today's Gospel reading of the night of Jesus' arrest, when he asks his sleepy disciples, "So, could you not keep awake [or "tarry" in older translations] with me for one hour?"

"Tarrying" seeks to offer an undeniable "yes". Through this practice, the faithful are able to write a new story. Rather than leaving Jesus lonely in his time of longing for spiritual companionship, he is met in the tarrying moment with a whole host of friends to accompany him. We are all called to "tarry" – watching and praying – with Jesus this Lent.

# Watch

Re-read Jesus' request of his disciples today – and notice how you respond to it.

# and pray

for all who are suffering alone, that they may be accompanied.

# God in darkness

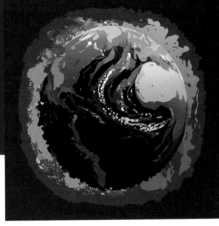

## Read

*"In the beginning... the earth was a formless void and the darkness covered the face of the deep, while a wind from God swept over the face of the waters."*

**Genesis 1.1-5**

There is a long and unfortunate convention – in the Christian tradition and far beyond it – of associating darkness and hiddenness only with evil, fear and danger. Simplistic notions that light exclusively represents truth, holiness, goodness, and godliness – and darkness always their opposites – limit the wonderful ways in which we can encounter the beauty and majesty of God across the diversity of our world.

At the start of Lent Christians often revisit the stories of God creating human beings "from the dust of the earth". Today's reading takes us back even further, to when – from "the formless void" – first the heavens and the earth are created, followed by human beings and all other creatures. This great work of God begins in the hidden and the unfathomable. Far from being bad, darkness is where God's most mighty work is done.

## Watch

Be open today to seeing darkness as somewhere God is at work.

## and pray

that you might discover God in new and unfamiliar places this Lent.

# Life-giving darkness

## Read

*"You make darkness, and it is night, when all the animals of the forest come creeping out."*

**Psalm 104.19-24**

Psalm 104 celebrates the wonders of God's world and praises God's wisdom in creating and ordering all things – including darkness.

As Selina Stone writes in *Tarry Awhile*, "Those of us who ever grew watercress at school will remember that it is in the darkness that particular forms of plant life grow ... It is in the darkness that we rest, our bodies recharge and our brains restore themselves ... Darkness is crucial to the development of particular species, which need space to hide away and hibernate. It is especially important for the young of various mammals (including humans) who grow in the darkness of the womb.

"Darkness ... is the exciting starting point of creation ... It is like a stage curtain, keeping things hidden until the appropriate time. Darkness ... is full of potential, expectation and anticipation."

# Watch

Look out for examples of God moving in darkness to bring life and growth.

# and pray

in the words of Psalm 104:
*"O Lord, how manifold are your works!
In wisdom you have made them all ..."*

# Unity

**The unity – the oneness – of the Christian faith is a key emphasis in Black Spirituality.**

However, from the earliest days, Christians have often lost sight of the God who St Paul declares "is above all and through all and in all".

We look this week at how all God's people might grow in unity and wholeness.

## Prayer for the Week

*Holy and mighty Trinity, teach us of your oneness. Give us grace to see the ways in which we reject the unity you desire in favour of division and conflict. Amen.*

# The oneness of God

## Read

"For in Christ all the fullness of God was pleased to dwell and through him God was pleased to reconcile to himself all things, whether on earth or in heaven..."

**Colossians 1.15-20**

The poetic language of Colossians 1 that describes the nature of Christ and the nature of God points to the deep truth of Christianity, also echoed in the other Abrahamic faiths, Judaism and Islam: God is one. God, alone, is God.

Christianity has wrestled with this for the first few centuries of the Church's life, and the ancient doctrine of the Trinity was developed: God is one God in three persons – Father, Son and Holy Spirit.

Our reading from Colossians brings us to the deep mystery that "in Christ all the fullness of God was pleased to dwell". African and African Caribbean spiritual traditions always begin from this place of the oneness of God. God's life is present in all of creation, God's very image within every human being.

## Watch

Be aware every person you meet today is loved by God, is made in God's image.

## and pray

for God's Holy Spirit to dwell within you and guide you.

# Reuniting all things

## Read

" ... for the earth will be full of the knowledge of the Lord as the waters cover the sea."

**Isaiah 11.6-9**

Yesterday we heard St Paul assert not only that God is one, but that God's deepest desire is for all things to be reconciled as one. This is a challenging statement that might – especially after a glance at today's news– seem too good to be true.

Today's reading from Isaiah's vision of the peaceable kingdom is perhaps one of the most hopeful parts of the Bible. Such passages remind us that God's endgame is peace across a violent and fractured world. Even the predator and prey lie down together in peace.

Black Spirituality insists that regardless of the harsh conditions of life, union and communion have the last word. Peace and healing lie deeper than pain and suffering. There will be a reconciliation of all things, and all time, in God. And, finally, all shall be well in the end.

## Watch

In the news and in your own life, look for any signs of hope, of harmony.

## and pray

for God's justice and for God's healing in our world.

# The dangers of dualism

## Read

*"There is one body and one Spirit ... one Lord, one faith, one baptism; one God and Father of all, who is above all and through all and in all."*

**Ephesians 4.1-6**

Ancient Greek and Roman thinking was strongly influenced by the notion that nature and life needed to be separated between the world that we can sense and the perfect world that we can only imagine: between the real world, and the ideal world.

The Letter to the Ephesians rejects this kind of "dualism", insisting on the reality of one God, one faith and one Christ. Yet dualistic thinking has caused problems for the Church from the outset. Accepting non-Jewish believers was the first hurdle of the Early Church. Later, European Christian missionaries to Africa and the Americas from the fifteenth century onwards treated indigenous cultures as idolatrous. Yet, these cultures were fertile grounds for the development of Christianity. Such "dualism" is dangerous because it creates division and conflict unnecessarily, hindering the good news of Jesus Christ.

## Watch

Notice any moments when you begin to see life in black-and-white terms.

## and pray

for the humility to accept grey and multi-coloured realities in life.

# Part of one unfolding story

## Read

"Now there was an Ethiopian eunuch, a court official of the Candace, queen of the Ethiopians, in charge of her entire treasury."

**Acts 8.26-39**

Found on the "wilderness road", an Ethiopian eunuch – a most unlikely character – learns the good news from Philip. He is devout. He is desiring to know the Hebrew Scriptures. But he is Black. He is a eunuch, which means that he is ritually impure according to ancient traditions. This is someone deemed illegitimate in every way, but nonetheless, one who is strategically part of the one unfolding Christian story begun in Acts.

When we consider the history of Christianity, it is easy to forget how it has Black and marginal beginnings, and how Black and African wisdom and insights have formed it through the writings of Tertullian, Abba Moses, Augustine of Hippo and many others. The Christian church had been established in Ethiopia for over a thousand years when the European missionaries we mentioned yesterday arrived – supposedly – to "Christianise" Africa.

## Watch

Take note of your reactions to the importance of Africa to the Early Church.

## and pray

for a deepening openness to the Spirit's movements in all people and places.

# Embracing the body

## Read

*"The gifts he gave were that some would be apostles, some prophets, some evangelists, some pastors and teachers, to equip the saints for the work of ministry, for building up the body of Christ ..."*

**Ephesians 4.7-16**

Oneness involves the body! Thanks in part to the legacy of "dualism" in Western thought we looked at yesterday, there has been a long history of seeing the body as less important than the spirit, or the material world as less valuable than the spiritual world. Christian theology has sometimes been charged with perpetuating deep suspicion or dislike for the body, seeing it as the place where sinfulness resides. But humans are embodied beings and true spirituality must include the body.

Today's reading from Ephesians describes the Christian community as "the body of Christ". Christ became incarnate (literally, "took on flesh") and became a human being to make God known to us. Christ lived, died and rose again in the body. When we say the Creed, we affirm our belief in "the resurrection of the body". Bodies matter to God, too!

## Watch

Think about the ways in which you see your body or treat your body.

## and pray

for faith lives that are more grounded in our God-given bodies.

# Sharing one bread

## Read

*"For as often as you eat this bread and drink the cup, you proclaim the Lord's death until he comes."*

**1 Corinthians 11.23-31**

Holy Communion is where we learn what it means to receive and to be the Body of Christ.

Selina Stone writes in *Tarry Awhile*, "To be invited around the Lord's table, is a privilege that none of us deserve. As we gather around the table that is not our own, at which we are guests, we are reminded ... of the reconciling work of Christ even while we tarry for this reconciliation in our experience. Of course, we experience moments of this reconciliation in the meantime ... Our hope is built up by these moments.

"The Eucharist ... is a time when we accept a gift that tells us a truth that even we might like to deny: that we are all children of God and siblings of one another ... it is through Christ's life, death and resurrection that we have been reconciled to God and to one another."

## Watch

Reflect on how Christians are united – but also sometimes divided – by the Lord's table.

## and pray

for deeper unity in the Body of Christ.

**Week 2**

# Movement

**This week we consider the theme of movement within the spiritual life.**

Waiting in darkness and uncertainty – a key aspect of Black Spirituality as we have seen – does not mean *not moving*. It means joining in with a God who is moving always within us, around us, and ahead of us.

God *is* movement. God *is* life.

---

## Prayer for the Week

*God of our ancestors, you have moved in generations past, and continue to move us in the present into your glorious future. Give us faith to trust you in the uncertainties of life. Amen.*

# Abraham: A model of movement

## Read

*"Now the Lord said to Abram, 'Go from your country and your kindred and your father's house to the land that I will show you.' "*

**Genesis 12.1–9**

Abram – whose name is later changed to Abraham – is held up as a symbol of faith or faithfulness throughout the Bible. God seems to have a way of calling people to do what is uncommon with the assurance that God is present in the moving and in the doing. God abundantly blesses and brings about his promises – however unlikely they seem to be at the outset.

It's in this painful move away from his father's home that God appears and promises Abram a land that he passes through. Abram does not understand how or when God's plan might be fulfilled, but nevertheless makes an altar to the Lord.

Black history is one where forced migration meant the leaving of the motherland, Africa. The unspeakable horror of this history remains unresolved, but out of this, much of the world has been blessed through Black Spirituality, ingenuity, creativity, and strength.

# Watch

What are the ways in which your life journeys have shaped your faith?

# and pray

for openness to God's unfolding plan for your life.

# Sarah: forced movement

## Read

*"When the officials of Pharoah saw Sarai, they praised her. And the woman was taken into Pharoah's house.*

**Genesis 12.10-20**

These ancestral stories are not only about men. They are also centrally about women, named and unnamed. Sarai (later called Sarah) moves to Egypt with her husband Abram to escape famine. This is a story of survival. But there is another dimension. Sarai is beautiful and Abram fears that he would be killed by the Pharaoh should it be found out that Sarai is his spouse. He puts his wife in danger by lying, saying that she is his sister. God preserves Sarai from this political game among men.

Tragically, forced migration remains a reality of our world as it was in these early stories of Genesis. Women – very often Black women – have too often borne the brunt of the pain and loss incurred during forced migration. It is often their faith that preserves not only themselves, but their partners and their children.

## Watch

Are there other women of the Bible, like Sarai, whose stories deserve more attention?

## and pray

for justice for women and children caught up in human trafficking.

# Shameful movement: Jacob

## Read

*"Your brother Esau is consoling himself by planning to kill you. Now therefore, my son, obey my voice; flee at once to my brother Laban in Haran."*

**Genesis 27.41-46**

The complex and difficult relationship between Isaac and Rebekah creates enmity between their sons, Esau and Jacob. Jacob is very much a trickster, seeking the love of his father, but supported and defended by his mother.

This is a fraught situation that leads to this ancestor fleeing his home. In this space of escape he finds the God of his forebears. Despite the deep shame that pursues Jacob, eventually his name is changed to Israel (Genesis 32.28). His shame becomes honour.

Black Spirituality is born out of the complex and difficult lives of Black people which often means that they have to leave their homes and their loved ones just to make a life elsewhere. Often, it is only their enduring faith in God that sustains them.

## Watch

Reflect on any journeys you might have undertaken out of shame or fear.

## and pray

for God's deep healing within the relationships of your life.

# Bethel: God moves closer

## Read

*"And the Lord stood beside Jacob and said, 'I am the Lord, the God of Abraham your father and the God of Isaac; the land on which you lie I will give to you ... "*

**Genesis 28.10-22**

Genesis 28 is a pivotal point in the story of Jacob, but also in the story of the ancient Hebrews. Movement is key to understanding this text. In Jacob's dream, a ladder appears between heaven and earth. Angels are ascending and descending. Jacob is moving – in fact, escaping – from one place to another. Amid all this, God comes close to him, and reveals himself, and blesses him. Jacob awakes and calls the place "Bethel", the House of God. He comes to see that the God of his ancestors moves with him, no matter where he might find himself.

God is present in our movement. The reality of forced migration for Black People across the globe has not meant the relinquishing of their faith. In fact, it's in the upheavals of life that we come to know God more clearly and powerfully.

# Watch

Think about the way migration and displacement of people has affected the history of faith.

# and pray

for deep encounters with God in the journeys of others you meet.

# Joseph: endurance

## Read

*"They said to one another, 'Here comes this dreamer. Come now, let us kill him and throw him into one of the pits ... and we shall see what will become of his dreams.'"*

**Genesis 37.12-28**

The Joseph narratives of Genesis are compelling and profoundly relatable to people who have been oppressed and must wrestle with the deepest of trials and betrayals. Joseph is sold into servitude by his brothers, out of jealousy. The family drama – from his grandfather Isaac through his father Jacob – finds its way into his own life. Joseph endures being betrayed and sold into slavery by his brothers, sexually harassed, falsely accused, imprisoned, ignored, and forgotten. In the midst of violence, trauma, and misfortune, he clings to God's gifts and presence in his life.

Joseph's faith and his coming to terms with his traumatic past ultimately brings him to a place of exaltation. The one despised becomes the hope for the very ones who betrayed him. Joseph is a powerful symbol for the faith of Black people, who have similarly endured oppression yet remained rooted in God.

# Watch

Reflect on any episodes in your own life that have involved trauma and adversity.

# and pray

for peace and healing over all these moments of your life.

# The God who moves

## Read

*"But Joseph said to them, 'Do not be afraid! Am I in the place of God? Even though you intended to do harm to me, God intended it for good ... "*

**Genesis 50.15-21**

We come to the end of the Book of Genesis. We also come to the conclusion of Joseph's story. What began in family trauma and betrayal, now ends in the most spectacular display of forgiveness and love between Joseph and his brothers. Joseph who was once a slave, then a prisoner, is now the most powerful person in Egypt apart from the Pharaoh.

There is a wider consideration. His forefather Abram once moved to Egypt because of famine. He is now the preserver of his kinsfolk who are in the midst of another famine.

An even wider lens reveals that all along, God had had been moving through their generations to bring about peacefulness and flourishing, despite the hardships, conflicts, and trauma. God is the God who moves – ahead of, alongside and behind his people.

# Watch

Remind yourself of moments of clarity and forgiveness in your life.

# and pray

for wisdom to discern God's larger purpose for your life.

**Week 3**

# Spirit

**This week we contemplate the work of the Spirit.**

The Spirit of God, or God as Spirit, is key to understanding Black Spirituality. God is spirit, and life, and movement, and shows up in every aspect of Black spiritual traditions.

## Prayer for the Week

*Great Spirit of God, you remain unquenched, and we dare not attempt to domesticate or limit you. Disrupt our false ideas and idolatries. Remake and renew us in your work of recreation. Amen.*

# The mighty Spirit

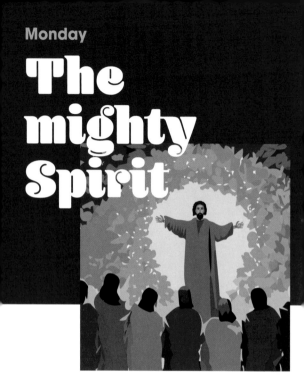

# Read

*"But you will receive power when the Holy Spirit has come upon you; and you will be my witnesses in Jerusalem, in all Judea and Samaria, and to the ends of the earth."*

**Acts 1.6-11**

Spirituality, or the presence and power of the spiritual world is emphasised in Black religious traditions, and other, mainly non-Western traditions. Black culture operates on the idea that the spiritual is intertwined with the physical and is inherently powerful.

This is true within the Biblical tradition. As Jesus ascends at the beginning of the Acts of the Apostles, he promises the coming of the Holy Spirit, not in a contained and inconspicuous way, but with power. The disciples would be empowered to be witnesses to Jesus and to become people they never imagined they would be. This is the same Spirit of God in operation at the beginning of Creation in Genesis 1, who hovers over the waters, bringing order out of chaos, bring life into being.

The Spirit of God is mighty!

# Watch

Look out for ways in which the Holy Spirit might be moving in the world today.

# and pray

for a deepening sense of the Holy Spirit in your everyday life.

# The disrupting Spirit

## Read

*"And suddenly from heaven there came a sound like the rush of a violent wind, and it filled the entire house where they were sitting."*

**Acts 2.1-13**

The beginning of Acts 2 records a decisive moment in the life of the Early Church. Some affectionately call it the birthday of the Church. But this is perhaps a rather a bland name for a truly dramatic event.

The Spirit comes in power and disrupts everything, fills everything, displaces everything! Disciples locked away in fear become emboldened. Those who could not speak were filled with a new energy, new giftings, and new fire. Peter, the one who was denies Jesus, becomes the first preacher. There is no shame here. There is simply a deep freedom in testifying to the great work of God in Christ Jesus.

Thanks to the disruptive power of the Spirit, those being hunted down by violent oppressors are now not afraid to disrupt the status quo to preach the truth of Jesus' resurrection from the dead. Ultimately, the Spirit always disrupts lies, violence and fear.

# Watch

Consider ways that the Holy Spirit might be disrupting your life and plans.

# and pray

for humility to allow to the Holy Spirit's power to reshape and redirect.

# The ancient Spirit

## Read

*"In the last days it will be, God declares, that I will pour out my Spirit upon all flesh, and your sons and your daughters shall prophesy ... "*

**Acts 2.14-24**

We are now at the heart of Peter's sermon on the Day of Pentecost. We come to a deep truth. The Spirit is none other than that ancient Spirit, the Spirit promised in the Book of the Prophet Joel from which Peter quotes. The plan was always for all to have access to the Spirit of God, without distinction. Most revivals and spiritual outpourings in Christian history have emerged from oppressed and marginalised communities and experiences.

When considering Black Spirituality, and especially the rise of Pentecostalism across the world that is connected to it, we see the same pattern. Black spiritual traditions are inherently Spirit-oriented (or "pneumatological"). This means that they prioritise the power and presence of the Spirit of God, and as such, they consistently remind us that the Spirit of God is ancient, and not contained by any religion or denomination.

# Watch

Note your thoughts and reflections on more expressive forms of Christianity.

# and pray

for a continued revival and outpouring of the Spirit within all our churches.

# The Holy Spirit

# Read

"Peter said to them, 'Repent, and be baptized every one of you in the name of Jesus Christ so that your sins may be forgiven; and you will receive the gift of the Holy Spirit."

**Acts 2.37-42**

In today's reading we encounter the first converts to Peter's message. We begin to see that they devote themselves to the teaching of the apostles, a central part of which is that upon repenting of their sins, believing in Jesus, and being baptised, they would receive the Holy Spirit.

This emphasis on the Holy Spirit in these early moments of Christian history is vital for later doctrinal developments. We now stand on centuries of reflection which have rested on the fact that the Holy Spirit is indeed the third person of the Trinity. However, there is more to be done and more to understand about how the Spirit operates in the world. Black Spirituality reminds us that "God is spirit, and those who worship him must worship in spirit and truth" (John 4.24).

# Watch

Consider how your understanding of the Holy Spirit has developed over time.

# and pray

for a stronger and deeper relationship with the Holy Spirit in your life.

# The indwelling Spirit

## Read

*"All who believed were together and had all things in common; they would sell their possessions and goods and distribute the proceeds to all, as any had need."*

**Acts 2.43-47**

The Spirit of God is mighty! Yes, the Spirit is Holy! But there is a deeper revelation about the Holy Spirit played out in the Acts of the Apostles. When we come to the end of Acts Chapter 2, the community of the first believers begin living in the world in a radically alternative way. They hold all things in common. They sell their possessions. They pray and worship together, breaking bread as Jesus taught them. They also were known for signs and wonders. Everyone was in awe of them.

What has made the difference here? It is the fact that this early Christian community is indwelled by the Holy Spirit. People of the Holy Spirit live alternatively, in a way that is distinctive and filled with grace. They seek unity and seek to rebuild where life is most broken. Their hearts are overfilled with love, despite the cold heartlessness of the world.

## Watch

Reflect on moments you might have felt the Holy Spirit within you.

## and pray

for a clearer sense of the indwelling of the Holy Spirit.

# Abiding with the Spirit

## Read

*"When the Spirit of truth comes, he will guide you into all the truth; for he will not speak on his own, but will speak whatever he hears, and he will declare to you the things that are to come."*

**John 16.1-15**

We end the week with words Jesus speaks to his disciples in the Upper Room on the night before his crucifixion and death. Jesus promises that he will send the "Advocate", the "Spirit of Truth" who will be active in the lives of the disciples and the Christians who will follow them. John's Gospel generally uses the word "abiding" to speak about relationship with God. Also, when reading the Acts of the Apostles, the entire book details the untameable movement of the Holy Spirit.

This "abiding" or "tarrying" with the Spirit – a key emphasis in Black Pentecostalism – requires us to be open to the unthinkable. For example, during the Azusa Street Revival in Los Angeles in 1906 to 1909, even white pastors came to learn from the Black leadership of the fellowship. Such openness to the Spirit's guiding is vital to our discipleship today.

# Watch

Take note of moments when you were surprised by life's outcomes.

# and pray

for greater openness to God's surprises in life.

# Quiet

**This week we consider moments in the lives of the prophets when – even amidst terrible suffering and oppression – they encounter the divine presence.**

Black Spirituality is ancient, and in many ways can be related to the themes and worldviews of the Hebrew prophets we will encounter this week.

---

## Prayer for the Week

*God of our wilderness and despair, when our chaos is too loud to hear you, lead us to the quiet place. Open the ears of our hearts to hear you in the deepest of ways. Amen.*

# Moses in the wilderness

## Read

"Moses ... came to Horeb, the mountain of God. There the angel of the Lord appeared to him in a flame of fire out of a bush ... the bush was blazing, yet it was not consumed."

**Exodus 3.1-12**

Moses is the model upon which all within the prophetic tradition in Scripture is based – even Jesus. We know the general story of Moses, and we place him within the political and economic situation of his time, but we must pay attention to the deep quiet within the text.

Moses spends his most powerful moments in the wilderness, or on a mountain top, alone with God.

In Exodus 3 he moves beyond the wilderness, and there he encounters God in the presence of a burning bush. At this point Moses is a shameful man, and in many ways someone who is lost and confused. But in this quiet moment, he comes to see what he never had before. He comes to learn the divine name, shared for the first time in Scripture. His path – and the path of God's people – is changed for ever.

## Watch

When and where have you felt God moving you beyond your comfort zone?

## and pray

for the curiosity and courage to seek God outside the ordinary.

# Elijah on the mountain

## Read

*"The Lord was not in the wind ... the Lord was not in the earthquake ... not in the fire; and after the fire a sound of sheer silence."*

**1 Kings 19.1-13**

Elijah is the other great prophet who – alongside Moses – makes it into the story of Jesus' transfiguration, appearing beside Jesus and talking with him.

In today's reading, Elijah is in deep distress. He is on the run from King Ahab and Queen Jezebel having defeated the many other false prophets who were loyal to them. He is afraid for his life, despite the display of divine power he has just witnessed. We learn from him that victory and defeat walk hand-in-hand in our spiritual lives, and that we often need a place to hear God most deeply, most clearly and most powerfully.

After climbing the mountain, Elijah finally hears God. Not in the fire, nor the earthquake, nor the wind, but – after waiting (or "tarrying") till they have passed – in the most profound quiet.

## Watch

Recall your moments of great triumph, and great defeat.

## and pray

for a sense of God's presence in all seasons of your life.

# Job on the dung hill

## Read

*"Job took a potsherd with which to scrape himself, and sat among the ashes."*

**Job 2.1-10**

The Book of Job is one of the oldest within the Hebrew Bible. It is a rich examination of the enduring question of how an all-loving and all-powerful God can allow undeserved suffering. Job finds himself on a dung hill, scraping his putrid sores. All he has and all that he owns has been taken away, violently and suddenly.

Most of the book is Job's deep questioning of why such evil and misfortune has befallen him. To make things worse, heaven is quiet. God does not answer him. Job does not know of the bargain over his life and faith God has made with Satan (whose name means "the accuser"). And when God answers Job, there is no justification given.

Black Spirituality has been shaped by experiences of injustice and undeserved suffering affecting whole communities for generation after generation. However, even when heaven is quiet, the faithful still learn to trust the goodness of God.

## Watch

Reflect on how you react when you feel unjustly wronged.

## and pray

for the courage to lay these feelings honestly before God.

# Jonah in the whale's belly

## Read

*"But the Lord provided a large fish to swallow up Jonah; and Jonah was in the belly of the fish for three days and three nights."*

**Jonah 1.1-4,7-17**

The Book for Jonah is a very interesting part of the Bible. It tells the intriguing story of a prophet who runs from God only to find himself in the belly of a whale, a quiet place.

While Jonah's three-day retreat inside the "great fish" is referred to in Matthew Chapter 12 by Jesus to explain his own coming death, burial and resurrection, it is Jonah's anger that is perhaps the most striking feature of the book as a whole. Job is sent to the chief city of a colonising power to declare judgement. He holds on to this long-awaited judgement, but at the last moment God grants mercy!

Jonah's anger then turns toward God. How dare God grant mercy when justice is needed? This is too often the dilemma facing peoples who have experienced oppression and persecution. Mercy and justice are hard to balance. Jonah remains trapped in his anger – unwilling to accept that mercy has a place alongside justice.

## Watch

When have you felt most angry against God?

## and pray

for a deeper faith to trust God's silence in the face of injustice.

# Jeremiah in a cistern

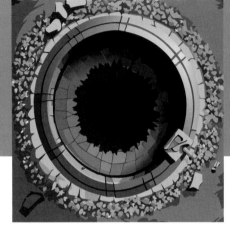

## Read

*"So they took Jeremiah and threw him into the cistern ... Now there was no water in the cistern, but only mud, and Jeremiah sank in the mud."*

**Jeremiah 38.1-13**

Jeremiah is the great prophet who experiences the exile into Babylon, and the complexity of life under colonial occupation. He has a word from God that is difficult, and he is faithful in proclaiming it. Those who dislike what he says puts him in a cistern, a place of no escape, to starve and die. Jeremiah – "the weeping prophet" – is made to be quiet through the plotting of his own people.

When the truth you speak is not heard, and attempts are made to silence you, it is heart-breaking. This has been the experience of Black people in racist and xenophobic societies. The silencing often leads to an inner rage. It is not only the mouth that is silenced, but one's identity, creativity and beauty. Jeremiah's ordeal offers an image of hope: he continued to speak God's truth, and time proved his words to be true.

## Watch

Recall moments when you felt profoundly unheard whilst speaking your truth.

## and pray

for courage to speak the truth in a world too often fashioned by lies.

# Jesus in the garden

## Read

*"Then Jesus came to the disciples and found them sleeping; and he said to Peter, "So, could you not stay awake with me one hour?"*

**Matthew 26.36-46**

Like those of the prophets who have come before him, Jesus' journey involves deep and quiet pain as much as it involves feats of power and miracles. We return today to the scene of Jesus in the quiet of the Garden of Gethsemane. He needs support, but his friends are asleep. He is in deep distress, his soul being "deeply grieved, even to death". This time of quiet is not quiet at all. It is the place of agony for Jesus, and we see his most vulnerable humanity on display.

Black Spirituality speaks powerfully of the aloneness and grief that attends the suffering soul. Places that have seen unspeakable suffering – former slave plantations, genocide camps – emit a deep quiet, because words cannot express the terrible histories they hold. But even in such places, though quiet, God is never absent.

## Watch

Reflect on how whole communities dwell in pain in our world.

## and pray

for deeper empathy and compassion within our churches.

# Healing

**We turn to the theme of healing which features strongly in Black Spiritual traditions.**

Healing is complex and multi-faceted – affecting mind and body, the physical and the spiritual, the individual and the community. This week we will focus on an important sequence of events from Mark's Gospel to help us explore this deep truth.

---

## Prayer for the Week

*O Holy One, you are the one who makes us whole again. We present to you our bodies, our minds, our spirits, our cultures and our communities. Heal us and send us out to tell others all that you have done for us. Amen.*

# Healing the spirit

## Read

*"And when he had stepped out of the boat, immediately a man out of the tombs with an unclean spirit met him."*

**Mark 4.35–5.2**

We will be focussing for most of this week on the story of Jesus' encounters in the country of the Gerasenes. It's a story that has many layers of meaning. On the face of it, though, it is an account of Jesus' healing a man "with an unclean spirit".

The Bible consistently points to the reality of a spiritual world beyond human understanding that affects the material. In today's passage the disciples witness Jesus' power over the physical world: "even the wind and the sea obey him." Jesus' next miracle – the exorcism of the man's demons – will show he is also Lord of the spiritual realm.

As we have seen, Black Spirituality emphasises the oneness of all things – the physical and the spiritual, the individual and the community. Jesus is able to heal the man's spirit – but the healing he offers goes far deeper and wider.

## Watch

What comes to mind when you think of the spiritual realm? Where do those images come from?

## and pray

for deeper attention to God's divine power, holiness, healing and love.

# Healing the mind

## Read

*"He lived among the tombs; and no one could restrain him any more, even with a chain ... "*

**Mark 5.1-4**

We might well prefer to interpret the man "with an unclean spirit" as being mentally and emotionally ill, rather than possessed. Today's reading describes someone "out of control" who has to be locked away from the community. He is a danger to himself and to others. Curiously, Jesus is the only one who treats the man as a human being. He speaks to him. Addresses him. And, as we will see later this week, asks his name.

Seeing another as a human being is important, especially when considering the treatment of those deemed mentally and emotionally unwell. In the UK, the scandalous fact is that individuals from UKME backgrounds are five times more likely to be detained under the Mental Health Act than white people.

This begs the question of who really needs the healing – and how?

## Watch

Notice how mental health is understood and treated in our world.

## and pray

for deeper compassion towards those who suffer mentally and emotionally.

# Healing the body

## Read

*"Night and day among the tombs and on the mountains he was always howling and bruising himself with stones."*

**Mark 5.5-8**

Bodies are important in this story. The description of the man among the tombs is graphic. He acts like an animal. He bruises himself. He has to be chained with iron. When he is finally delivered, the demons are sent into pigs – another "unclean" and despised animal. Clearly, this man is in need of healing in body, mind and spirit.

But the allusion to bodies being restrained, chained and abused carries deeper significance. Scapegoated people throughout history – those seen as "other" by the majority – become the target of dehumanising violence. For centuries, systems of control and abuse "demonised," vilified, enslaved and brutalised Black bodies.

Again, this story prompts the question: who is really in need of healing? This man is a victim of a system that is violent and determined not to see his humanity, his value – certainly not as Jesus does.

## Watch

Take note of the ways broken bodies often point to violent systems.

## and pray

for systems of justice that seek to heal all aspects of people's lives.

# Healing society

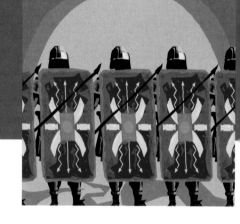

## Read

*"... for he had often been restrained with shackles and chains, but the chains he wrenched apart, and the shackles he broke in pieces, and no one had the strength to subdue him."*

**Mark 5:1-20**

This healing miracle cannot be understood in full without paying attention to the clues in Mark's text. The name of the man's demons – "Legion" – is the name for the largest military unit of the Roman army. There was Roman colonial outpost near Gerasa (or Gadara as Matthew refers to it). The shackling with iron was a particular Roman military method.

When we peel back the layers of the text we see Jesus encountering a community under occupation – from oppressive earthly and spiritual forces. Mark leaves us to discover that the society in which both the man and the community reside needs healing. The 'demon' here is systemic, hidden and deeply rooted.

Systemic evils such as racism, homophobia, misogyny and xenophobia often lie deep and hidden. Jesus offers the kind of healing that operates at the deepest level.

# Watch

Reflect on military conflicts across our world.

# and pray

for the cultures and histories of violence to cease.

# Rejecting the source of healing

## Read

*"Then they began to beg Jesus to leave their neighbourhood."*

**Read Mark 5.14-20**

By the end of the story, the troubled man is at peace, healed and proclaiming how much Jesus has done for him. But the community – perhaps stirred up by the swineherds who have lost out financially by the drowning of the pigs – is now begging Jesus to leave their country. If we allow ourselves to see the irony of it, Jesus – even though he had brought healing and deliverance – is exorcised from the community.

This healing miracle is not only about the social, political, and cultural ill-health of the Roman colonial world. It is also a mirror to all our communities, including communities of faith. Christian communities must always be mindful of the ways in which we can reinforce injustice, inequality and division - if we do not reflect on and challenge them. We cannot bring Christ's healing to others if we do not recognise our own need of it.

# Watch

Take note of the ways you find healing difficult.

# and pray

for wisdom to recognise that all of us are in need of healing and forgiveness.

# Reaching for healing

## Read

*"She had heard about Jesus, and came up behind him in the crowd and touched his cloak, for she said, 'If I but touch his clothes, I will be made well.' "*

**Mark 5.21-34**

We saw Jesus' healing power rejected by the people of Gerasa yesterday. But the miracle that immediately follows it – Jesus' healing of the woman suffering from haemorrhages – shows us someone determined to receive it.

Selina Stone writes in *Tarry Awhile*, "this story is as much about this woman's determination as it is about the power of Jesus. Healing does not fall into her lap; it is passing by, and she has to literally be ready to grab it …

"Was God working in her, to get her to this point, where she was willing to venture beyond the limits of tradition to fight for her own life? Did her healing begin as she began to recognise that her life mattered, and that she deserved to be well? … Her mind and spirit are healed enough, so that her body might also be."

---

# Watch

Reflect on moments when you missed opportunities for healing and transformation.

---

# and pray

for the courage to "grab" future moments and opportunities for healing.

---

# Weeping

**Tears – whether silent or aloud – flow from the deepest of human experiences.**

Many of these are tears of heartbreak and despair, tears of the abandoned or forsaken. But tears also convey deep love.

We will pay attention to the tears shed by Jesus and those around him during this Holy Week.

---

## Prayer for the Week

*We come to you, the One who weeps with us. Through your sorrows, soothe our deepest despair; through your sufferings, draw us into the comfort of your divine embrace. Amen.*

# Jesus Weeps

## Read

*"As Jesus came near and saw the city, he wept over it ... "*

**Luke 19.41-44**

Chapter 19 is pivotal in Luke's Gospel narrative. It records Jesus' triumphal entry into Jerusalem. He rides through the crowds on a donkey, a sign of humility and servanthood. He goes to the temple and turns over the tables of the money changers, declaring that God's house should be a house of prayer, not a den for thieves and robbers. However, between these two dramatic scenes is a moment where Jesus weeps over the city. He weeps for the judgement and pain which will follow the people's rejection of him.

Luke's Jesus is quite the weeper – deeply empathic, and in touch the with pain of those around him. He is the embodiment of a God who is not distant, but deeply weeps for his children. This is perhaps the powerful image of the Jesus within Black Spirituality: the God who weeps with the forsaken, the broken and the crucified.

# Watch

Notice what reactions you have to the idea that Jesus weeps.

# and pray

for a faith that that is filled with empathy and concern for our neighbour.

# Judas weeps

## Read

*"Judas said, 'I have sinned by betraying innocent blood.' Throwing down the pieces of silver in the temple, he departed; and he went and hanged himself."*

**Matthew 27.3-10**

Judas takes his own life. This is a vivid and uncomfortable part of Scripture that isn't often really expounded on. There is no explicit mention of him weeping but only an explanation of his deep guilt and remorse over betraying Jesus. But this is in keeping with such shattering experiences. Often the tears are silent. The despair is penetrating, and the sorrow is inexpressible.

Suicide is taboo in most societies. Often it is discussed in ways that blame the victim. Little understanding and compassion are given for the situations that precede it, especially the deep feelings of guilt and shame. This is also something taboo in Black communities, but in reflecting honestly on the traumas of Black history, there can be some understanding here.

What is also clear is that Jesus does not condemn or refuse to forgive Judas. There was space for Judas, too, even after his betrayal.

## Watch

Take note of the ways in which suicide is talked about in our world.

## and pray

for deeper compassion for victims and families in such situations.

# Peter weeps

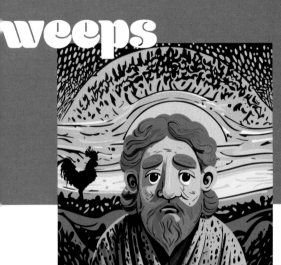

## Read

*"Then Peter remembered what Jesus had said: "Before the cock crows, you will deny me three times." And he went out and wept bitterly."*

**Matthew 26.69-75**

Peter is a coward! Jesus has predicted Peter's denial of him when called to account. Peter now sees it come true and runs away weeping bitterly. Unlike Judas, he weeps openly. And, also unlike Judas, he has a chance to be redeemed later, as described in John Chapter 21. Peter becomes the leading disciple in the Acts of the Apostles, and particularly the one preaching the first sermon at Pentecost in Acts Chapter 2. Nonetheless, like Judas, his tears also come from love. They both loved their teacher, their friend, and their Lord. Both their hearts were broken during Jesus' passion. Tears suggest the intensity and depth of the relationship.

Black Spirituality does not shy away from tears. Tears, whether bitter or joyful, are signs of love and devotion. Weeping together knits us closer to each other and into the heart of the God who wept and suffered for our sake.

# Watch

Notice your relationship with your emotions, especially your own tears.

# and pray

for the strength to accept and express difficult emotions in healthy ways.

# Mary weeps

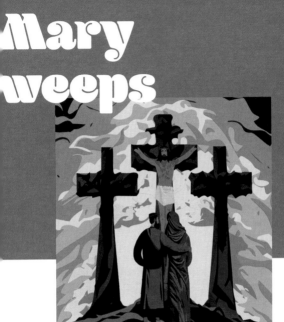

## Read

*"When Jesus saw his mother and the disciple whom he loved standing beside her, he said to his mother, 'Woman, here is your son.' "*

**John 19.16b-27**

Mary weeps. Mary and the women closest to Jesus follow along as Jesus is moved towards Golgotha. This is a painful road – the *Via Dolorosa* – not only for Jesus, but for his mother too. She stands beneath the cross to the bitter end. Mary has known that this deep pain would come, as prophesied by Simeon when she and Joseph presented their child in the temple (in Luke Chapter 2). The knowledge of his impending death is a burden she has long carried.

Many Black mothers have carried within their souls the truth that their children – especially their sons – were likely to be killed at an early age, or jailed, victims of systemic injustice. They have had to stand by when their children have been crucified by systems of violent racism. They, like Mary, have had simply to abide – clinging to love, enveloped in tears – to the bitter end.

## Watch

Become aware of mothers weeping for their children across our violent world.

## and pray

for a worldwide sorrow for the killing of innocents and children.

# All creation weeps

## Read

"At that moment the curtain of the temple was torn in two, from top to bottom. The earth shook, and the rocks were split."

**Matthew 27.45-54**

The moment of Jesus' death in Matthew's Gospel is dramatic – not only for Jesus himself, but for the physical world. Darkness covers the whole land ... the curtain of the temple is torn in two ... the earth shakes and the rocks split ... the tombs open and the dead are raised to life appearing to many" and it is all described as "an earthquake".

This is a way of describing the overwhelming experience of the created order. The earth weeps. Death and the grave are beside themselves. This is a death that shakes the universe. Indigenous spiritualities and Black spiritual traditions that are still close to creation and the environment know that there is a connectedness of all things. On Good Friday, Jesus dies on the cross. All of creation groans, and all of history weeps.

# Watch

Spend time in silence today contemplating Jesus' death on the cross.

# and pray

for a deeper and larger understanding of Jesus' life and death.

# We shall weep

## Read

*"For at that time there will be great suffering, such as has not been from the beginning of the world until now, no, and never will be."*

**Matthew 24.15-27**

Matthew Chapter 24 is a difficult part of the Gospel full of apocalyptic predictions. Many have used it to predict the present age and the future in definitive ways. It is tempting to use it to predict, for example, the coming of the Son of Man, and the how the end time judgement will take place. However, the chapter ends by stating that all should be prepared since the Son of Man will come "at an unexpected hour" (verse 44). Nonetheless, it does warn that what will certainly take place is "weeping and gnashing of teeth" (verse 51).

These difficult passages, like apocalyptic passages generally, remind us of the utter reality of the human condition. Deep suffering is a part of life. Black spiritual traditions remind us that trial and pain are part of being human. But they also remind us that weeping is not the final experience.

## Watch

Call to mind places and people in the world today who are in the grip of weeping and grief.

## and pray

for glimpses of the new heaven and earth God promises to bring about.

Easter Day

# Morning

*Alleluia. Christ is risen.*
*He is risen indeed. Alleluia.*

# Read

*"As the disciples were gathering in Galilee, Jesus said to them, 'The Son of Man is going to be betrayed into human hands, and they will kill him, and on the third day he will be raised.' And they were greatly distressed."*

**Matthew 17.22-23**

When reading through Matthew's Gospel we may wonder why the disciples were surprised by Jesus' crucifixion and resurrection. Jesus had been preparing his disciples along the journey to Jerusalem. He utters the same words, almost verbatim, three times (in Matthew Chapters 16, 17 and 20). Jesus tried to make things as clear as possible for his disciples. It is reminder that even the Lord of life must endure darkness. But the darkness and despair foretold is hard to conceptualise until it arrives. Within seasons of darkness and despair resurrection is unthinkable.

Let us give the final word to Selina Stone, whose book *Tarry Awhile* exploring Black Spirituality has inspired these reflections:

"This is what it means for us to be people of the resurrection. We inhabit a world that is not yet what it will be, as people who continue to be formed into the likeness of Christ who embodied life and love in their fullness. The scars we bear are not cause for shame, nor must they define us in our entirety. They remind us of the work of God which continues to be needed in the world and in each of us, as we tarry ever more, for the reign of God to be made known among us in justice and peace."

# Watch

Spend some time noticing how these forty days of watching and praying, tarrying and reflecting have helped to deepen your faith.

# and pray

Holy God, grant us the faith to trust you in times of struggle. Give us courage to dwell with you, knowing that you will bring us to new life. Amen.

# Going Further

**Jesus Christ is at the heart of our vision for the Church of England.**

**Where will a life centred on Christ take you?**

We hope you have enjoyed this *Watch and Pray* journey. Here are some ways you might want to travel further in the faith in the days and month ahead:

**Join with others in worship and service at your local church.** Find thousands of services and events, groups and activities taking place near you via **AChurchNearYou.com**

**Sign up for future Church of England reflections.** Visit **churchofengland.org** to sign up for future campaigns and resources – including Advent and Christmas reflections. It's free to sign up for emails and you can easily opt out at any time.

**Explore God in everyday life with *Everyday Faith*.** *Everyday Faith* provide resources for individuals and churches to help them find and follow God in everyday life. Visit **churchofengland.org/everyday-faith** to find out more.

**Find out more about the work of the Church of England's Racial Justice Unit (RJU).** The RJU is working across the Church to address racial injustice and to promote diversity and inclusion. Visit **churchofengland.org/racial-justice** to find out more.